# A Visit to the UNITED KINGDOM

NORTH AMERICA

SOUTH AMERICA

UNITED KINGDOM

EUROPE

AFRICA

ASIA

AUSTRALIA

## Rachael Bell

Heinemann LIBRARY

First published in Great Britain by Heinemann Library,
Halley Court, Jordan Hill, Oxford OX2 8EJ,
a division of Reed Educational and Professional Publishing Ltd.

Heinemann is a registered trademark of Reed Educational & Professional Publishing Limited.

OXFORD   MELBOURNE   AUCKLAND
JOHANNESBURG   BLANTYRE   GABORONE
IBADAN   PORTSMOUTH (NH) USA   CHICAGO

Designed by AMR
Illustrations by Art Construction
Printed and bound in Hong Kong/China by South China Printing Co.

03 02 01 00 99
10 9 8 7 6 5 4 3 2 1

ISBN 0 431 08340 1

**British Library Cataloguing in Publication Data**

Bell, Rachael
  A visit to the UK
  1. Great Britain – Juvenile literature
  I.Title II.The UK
  941

**Acknowledgements**
The Publishers would like to thank the following for permission to reproduce photographs:
Ace Photo Agency: Geoff Smith p 8; Aviemore Photographic: p 27; Bubbles: Pauline Cutler p 14; Collections: Gena Davies p 6, Roger Scruton p 12; Images Colour Library: pp 5, 7; J. Allan Cash Ltd: pp 11, 15, 17, 19, 21, 22, 23, 24, 26, 29; Link: Orde Eliason p 16, Sue Carpenter p 25; Shakespeare's Globe: p 28; The Anthony Blake Photo Library: Gerrit Buntrock p 13; The Skyscan Photolibrary: p 10; Tony Stone Images: Penny Tweedie p 20; Trip: P Rauter p 9, C Kapolka p 18.

Cover photograph reproduced with permission of Tony Stone Images/Peter Cade.

Every effort has been made to contact copyright holders of any material reproduced in this book. Any omissions will be rectified in subsequent printings if notice is given to the Publisher.

Any words appearing in bold, **like this**, are explained in the Glossary.

# Contents

# The United Kingdom

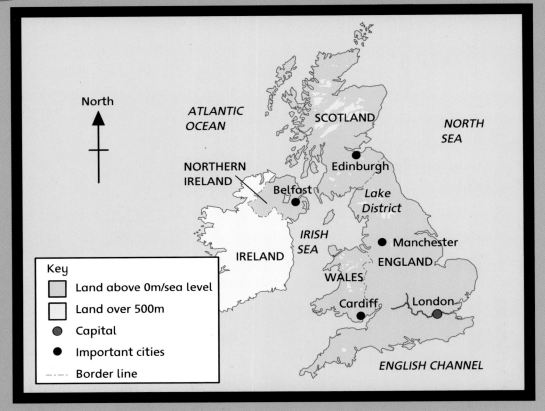

North

ATLANTIC OCEAN

SCOTLAND

NORTH SEA

NORTHERN IRELAND

Edinburgh

Belfast

Lake District

IRISH SEA

IRELAND

Manchester

ENGLAND

WALES

Cardiff

London

**Key**
- Land above 0m/sea level
- Land over 500m
- Capital
- Important cities
- Border line

ENGLISH CHANNEL

The United Kingdom is made up of a large island called Great Britain and hundreds of little islands.

Most people call the United Kingdom 'the UK', for short. There are four different areas in the UK that used to be separate countries. These are England, Northern Ireland, Scotland and Wales.

# Land

The north of the country has mountains and deep valleys and lakes. In the south, there are gentle hills with wide rivers, where it is easier to grow crops.

There is lots of rain on the high land in the west of the country. Rain makes the grass and plants grow well there.

# Landmarks

The Giant's Causeway in Northern Ireland is a strange **volcanic** rock on the coast. **Legend** says it was a giant's road that was built to step over the sea into Scotland.

London, the **capital** of the UK, has many famous buildings. The Tower of London was once a prison castle. Today, many **tourists** go to see its **keepers** and the **crown jewels**.

# Homes

Most people in the UK live in houses
in towns or cities. Many of these houses
were built over 100 years ago.

Some people live in blocks of flats. New ones are being built and some empty old buildings in city centres are being made into flats.

# Food

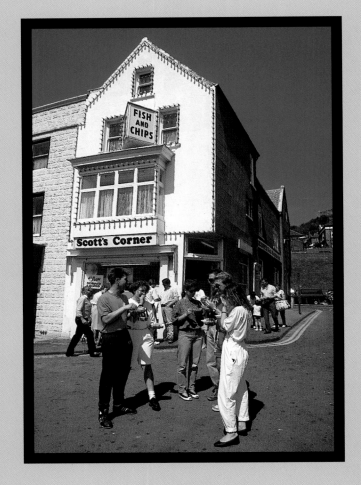

You will find a fish and chip shop in every town. Because the UK is an island, fishermen supply fresh fish throughout the year. Chips are a popular snack.

Different parts of the UK have their own special dishes but many families enjoy a **traditional** Sunday lunch. This is a big piece of cooked meat, which is eaten with potatoes, other vegetables and **gravy**.

# Clothes

Many famous **fashion designers** come from the UK. Young people enjoy wearing clothes made by these top designers. Sports clothes are also very popular.

One of the **traditional** clothes in the UK is the tartan kilt. This is a checked, wool skirt worn by Scottish men and women on special occasions.

# Work

Seven out of ten people in the UK work in a service industry. This means that they work in transport, **education**, health and leisure, or money-related work.

Most other people work in industry. This means that they help to make or build things, like cars. Very few people work in farming in the UK.

# Transport

The London Underground was opened
over 100 years ago and used **steam trains**!
Now it uses electricity, and three million
people travel on it every day.

Most people travel to work by car and goods are transported by lorry. This means that the roads and motorways are very busy and there is a lot of **pollution**.

# Language

English is the most spoken language in the world. But in the UK, one person might not understand another because each area has a different **accent**.

In the UK about one million people speak Welsh and some people speak **Gaelic**. Some people speak other languages because their parents or grandparents came from other countries.

# School

Children have to go to school from the age of 5 until they are 16. They study science, geography, history, English, music, maths, art and physical education.

Most schools are free and children from the local area go there. Some schools charge parents money and sometimes the children can sleep there, too.

# Free time

Many famous sports have come from the
UK, like football, tennis and cricket.
Children play these both in and out of
school. Most adults prefer to just watch!

Many people enjoy being outdoors.
Some go to the beach in summer. Others
go walking or cycling in the mountains
in the Lake District or Scotland.

# Celebrations

The biggest celebration of the whole year is Christmas. The streets are lit with Christmas lights. People buy presents for each other and eat special Christmas food.

Another special celebration in Scotland is Burns' Night. People wear tartan clothes, and eat a special food called haggis. They listen to **bagpipe** music.

# The Arts

The UK is famous for its theatre. **Shakespeare's** plays are very well-known all around the world. Also, there are many theatres and theatre festivals.

The UK has many musicians and pop groups. In Wales the Eisteddfod festival is a big competition for people who sing, write poetry or play music.

# Factfile

| | |
|---|---|
| **Name** | The full name of the UK is the United Kingdom of Great Britain and Northern Ireland. |
| **Capital** | The **capital** city of the United Kingdom is London. |
| **Language** | Most people speak English, but some also speak Welsh or Gaelic. |
| **Population** | There are about 58 million people living in the United Kingdom. |
| **Money** | The English have the pound (£), which is divided into 100 pence. The Irish pound is called a punt. Scotland and Wales also have their own coins and bank notes. |
| **Religion** | There are many Christians in the United Kingdom, as well as Muslims, Sikhs, Hindus, Jews and Buddhists. |
| **Products** | The United Kingdom produces oil and gas, wheat and other foods, chemicals, cars and other transport machinery. |

## Words you can learn

These words are Welsh Gaelic.

| | |
|---|---|
| diolch (DEE-olkh) | thank you |
| bore da (boh-re-DAR) | good morning |
| nos da (norse-dar) | good night |
| hwyl fawr (hooeel-vowr) | goodbye |
| ie (EE-eh) | yes |
| na (nar) | no |

# Glossary

| | |
|---|---|
| **accent** | a different way of saying the same word |
| **bagpipes** | a musical instrument that you blow. It has pipes and a bag to collect the air |
| **capital** | the city where the government is based |
| **crops** | the plants that farmers grow and harvest (gather) |
| **crown jewels** | the crowns and special jewels worn by the Queen of Great Britain |
| **education** | anything to do with teaching children or adults |
| **fashion designers** | people who draw ideas for clothes which are then made |
| **Gaelic** | the ancient language of the people who first lived in Ireland, Wales, and Breton in France |
| **gravy** | meat juices that are made into a sauce |
| **keepers** | people who wear special clothes and protect a building |
| **legend** | a well-known, old story |
| **pollution** | dirt and poisons that fill the air, usually made by car and lorry engines |
| **Shakespeare** | a man who lived over 400 years ago. He wrote plays and poems that are still popular today |
| **steam train** | an old type of train that burned coal to make steam which made the engine work |
| **tourists** | people who travel to other places for holidays or to see the sights |
| **traditional** | the way things have been done or made for a long time |
| **volcanic** | a type of rock that has melted and is pushed out from beneath the Earth's surface |

# Index

Book No.

Books are loaned for a three week period. Books not in demand may be renewed by telephone, post or in person. **At libraries with a computerised system,** please quote the number on your membership card, **or** the number on the computer label on the inside back cover of the book. **At libraries with a manual system,** please quote (1) the last date stamped on the date label; (2) the book number and the author's name; (3) your name and address.

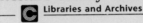

**Cheshire County Council**
**Libraries and Archives**